THIS JOURNAL BELONGS TO:
Mom
Daughter
Name:
Name:
We start this journey with:
AF417863

Today marks the beginning of a special journey together – a journey of discovery, connection, and meaningful conversations through this journal. This is more than just a place for words; it's a space where you can share your thoughts, dreams, and moments that bring you closer as mother and daughter. As you fill these pages, remember that every entry is a step toward understanding each other more deeply and creating memories that will last a lifetime. Here's to the start of something truly amazing – your shared story.

About Mom

Name: _______________________________

Age: _______________________________

Hair Color: _______________________________

Eye Color: _______________________________

Height: _______________________________

Favorite Color: _______________________________

Favorite Animal: _______________________________

A list of names my Daughter uses to refer to me:

____

____

____

About Mom

Here is a list of words I would use to describe my Mom:

____

____

____

____

Here is list of things she says all the time:

____

____

____

____

About Me

Name: _______________

Age: _______________

Hair Color: _______________

Eye Color: _______________

Height: _______________

Favorite Color: _______________

Favorite Animal: _______________

A list of names Mom uses for me:

____

____

____

About Me

Mom, list the words you would use to describe me:

____

____

____

____

List the things I say all the time:

____

____

____

____

____

Mom and Me

Mom and Me

Here is a silly song we wrote:

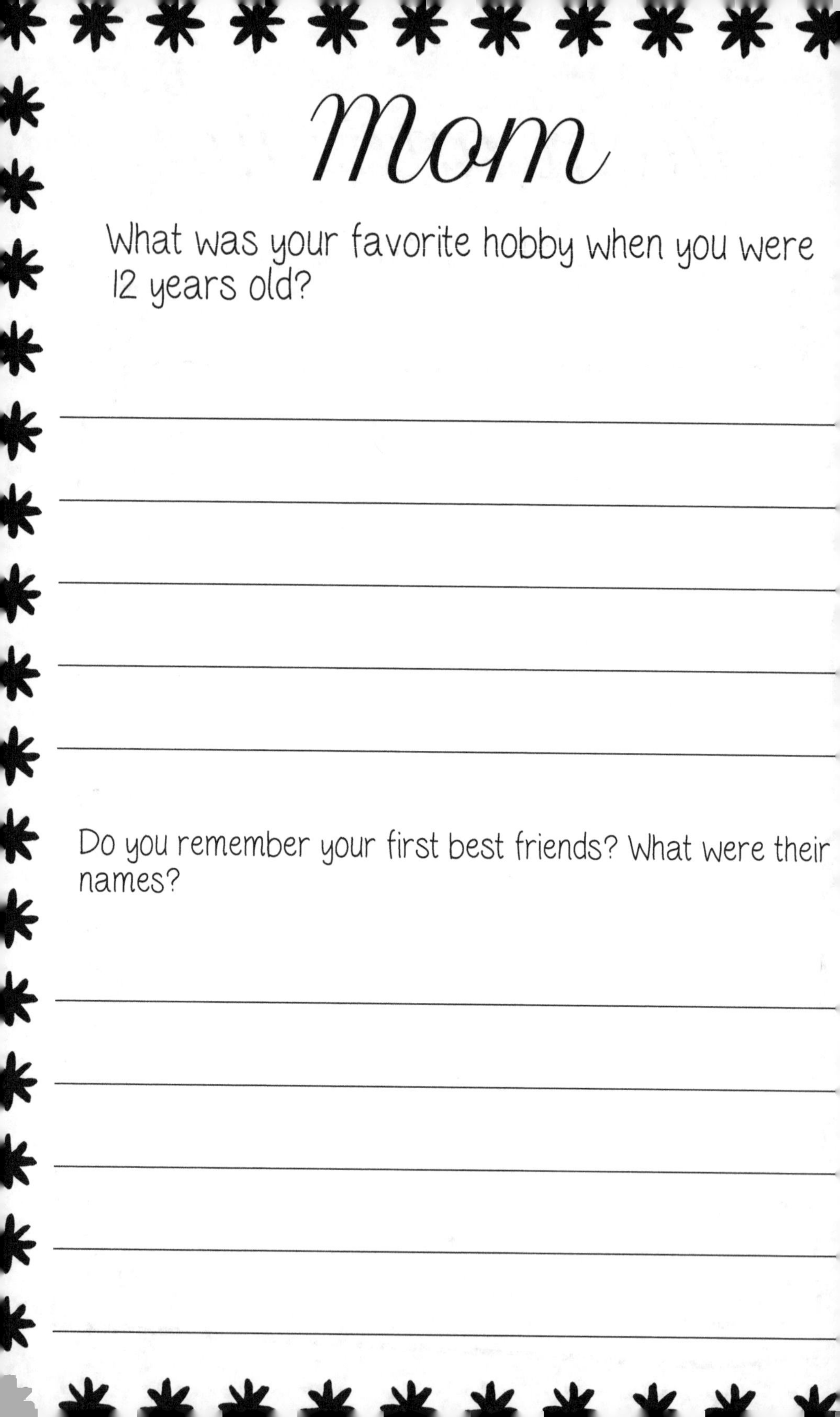

Mom

What was your favorite hobby when you were 12 years old?

Do you remember your first best friends? What were their names?

Daughter

What do you enjoy doing most after school?

What is your biggest dream for the future?

Mom

What were your dreams when you were my age?

What is your favorite childhood book?

Daughter

What makes you feel the happiest?

____

____

____

____

What books do you like to read?

____

____

____

____

If you could describe yourself in three words, wh[at]
would they be?

What makes you feel calm?

Mom

Did you ever keep a secret diary?

What did you love doing most during summer vacations as a kid?

Daughter

What makes you feel safe?

____

____

____

____

What are your favorite things to do on weekends?

____

____

____

____

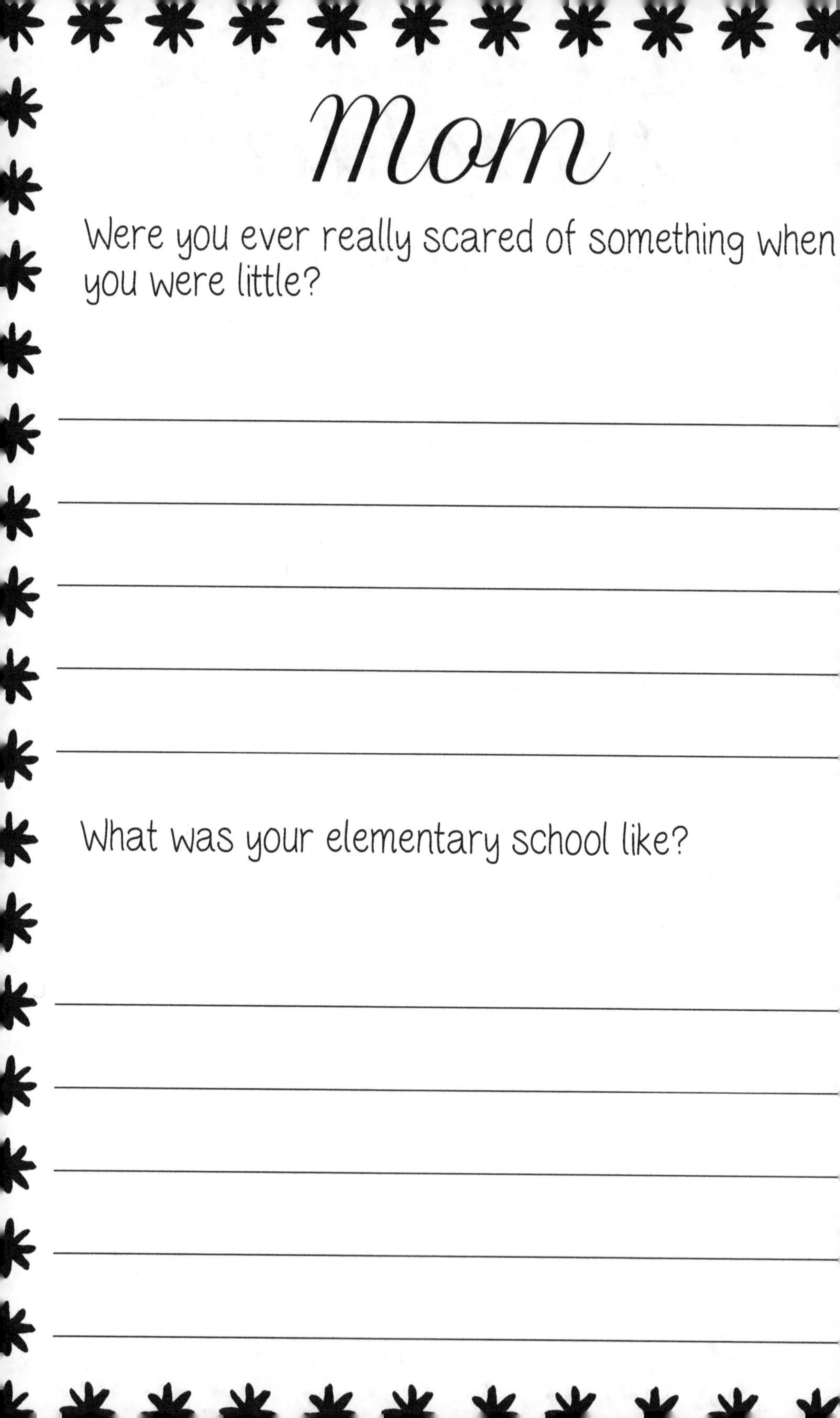

Mom

Were you ever really scared of something when you were little?

What was your elementary school like?

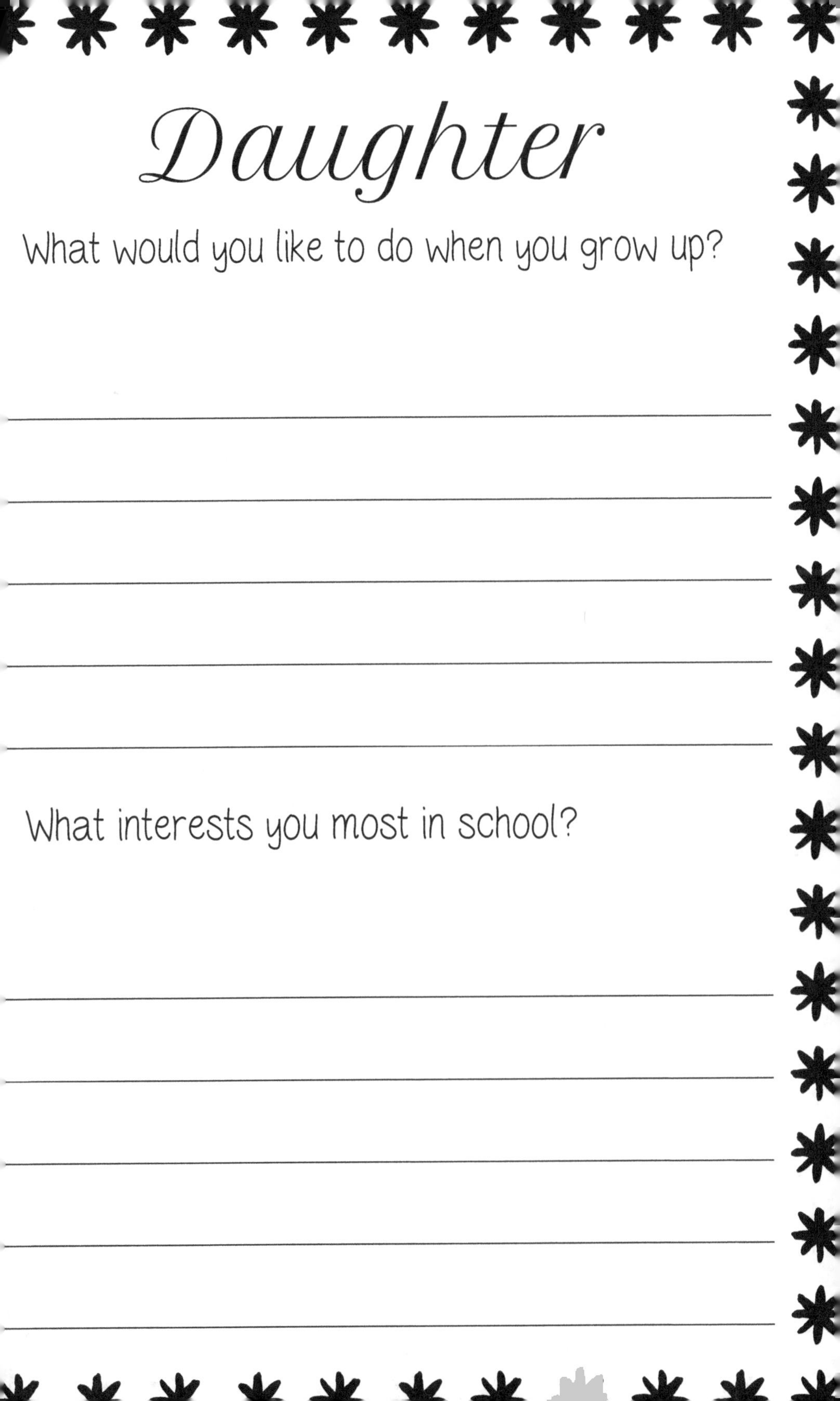

Daughter

What would you like to do when you grow up?

____

____

____

____

What interests you most in school?

____

____

____

____

What is your favorite memory of our time together?
ME
MOM

If you could change one thing in your life, what would it be?

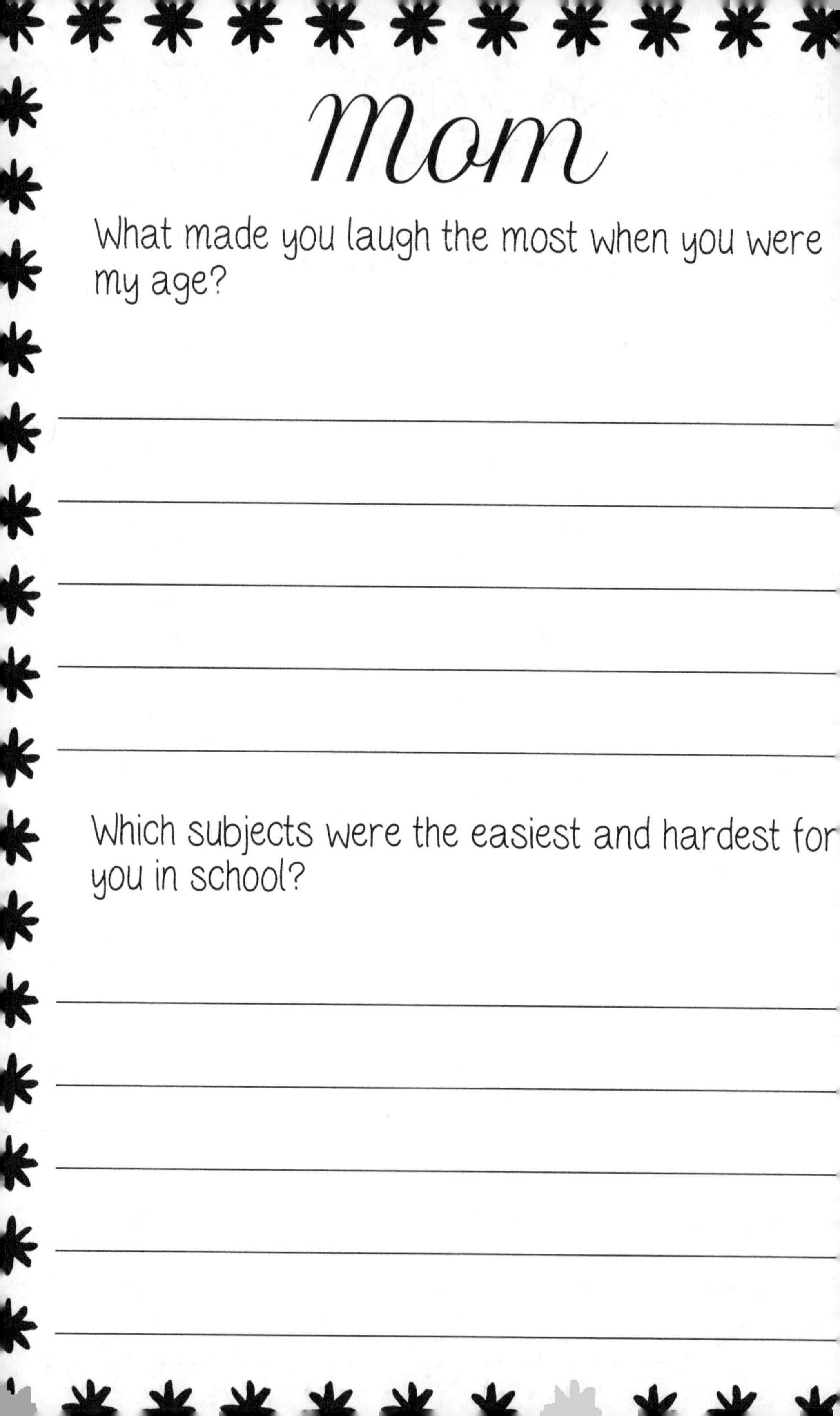

Mom

What made you laugh the most when you were my age?

Which subjects were the easiest and hardest for you in school?

Daughter

Do you have any dreams that you'd like to share with me?

____

____

____

____

____

What do you like most about our time together?

____

____

____

____

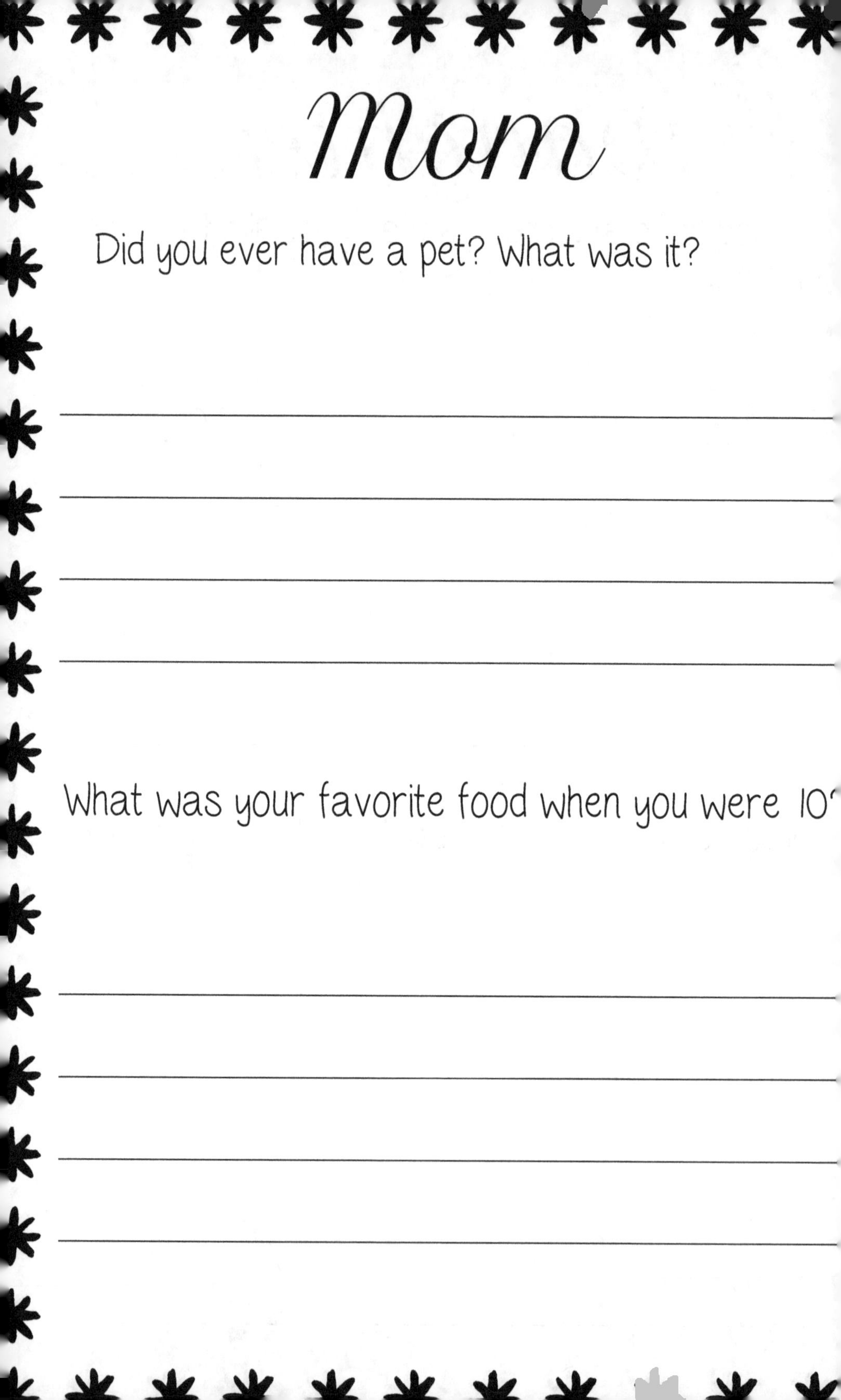

Mom

Did you ever have a pet? What was it?

____

____

____

____

What was your favorite food when you were 10?

____

____

____

Daughter

What are your favorite movies or TV shows?

____

____

____

____

What makes you feel sad?

____

____

____

____

What is your biggest travel dream?
ME
MOM

What do you like most about yourself?

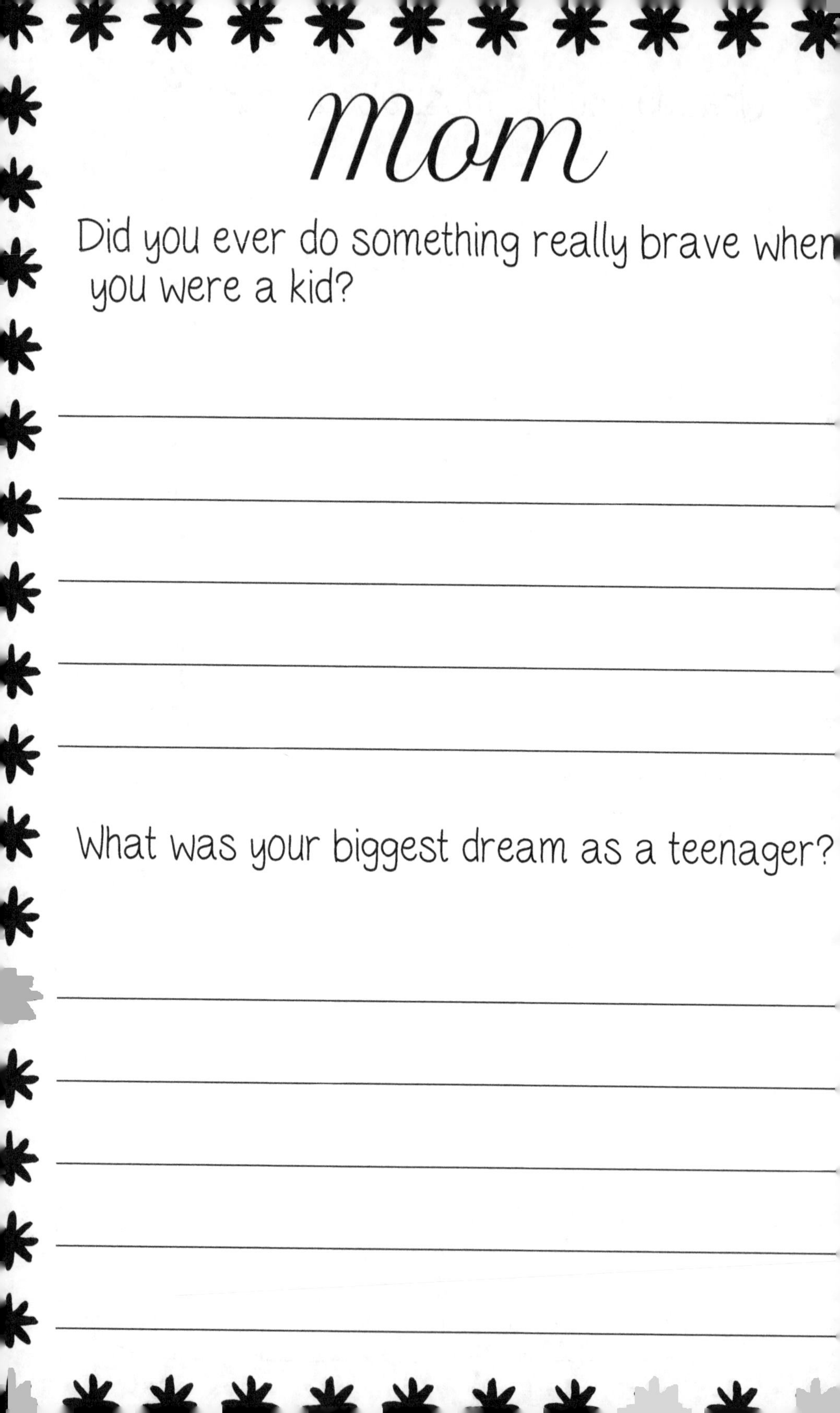

Mom

Did you ever do something really brave when you were a kid?

____

____

____

____

What was your biggest dream as a teenager?

____

____

____

____

Daughter

What are your favorite songs?

Is there something you wish I knew about you that you've never told me?

Mom

What did your room look like when you were little?

____

____

____

____

Did you have a special place you went to calm down?

____

____

____

____

Daughter

What makes you feel special?

Who is your best friend, and why?

What is your favorite memory with your friends
ME
MOM

What makes you feel safe?

Mom

What were your favorite outdoor games?

What's your happiest memory from childhood?

Daughter

What do you love doing most with the family?

____

____

____

____

What is your biggest challenge in school?

____

____

____

____

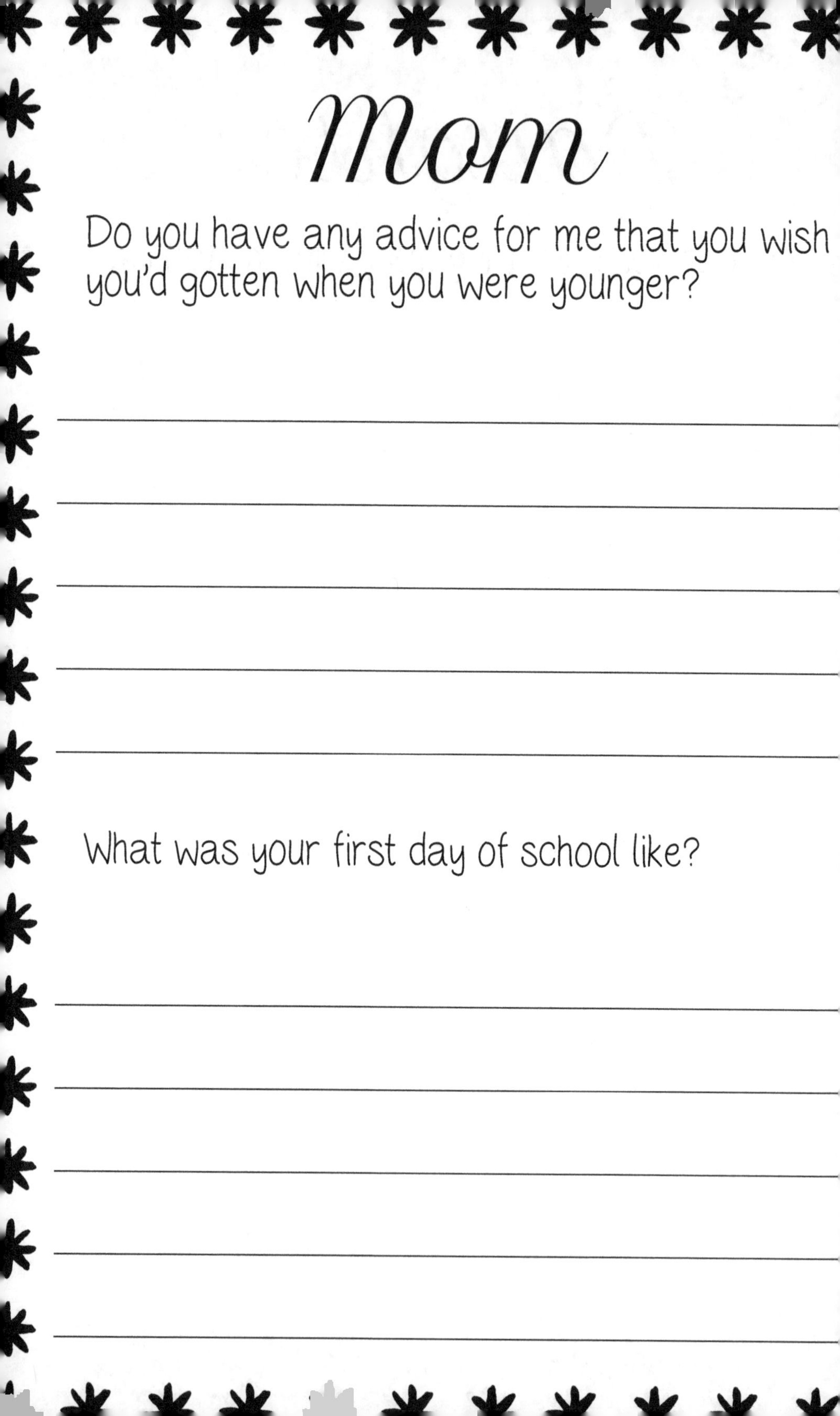

Mom

Do you have any advice for me that you wish you'd gotten when you were younger?

What was your first day of school like?

Daughter

What would you like to try that you've never
done before?

____

____

____

____

What's your best memory from a vacation?

____

____

____

____

What is your favorite dish that we eat together
ME
MOM

If you could spend one day in the past, when would it be?
MOM
ME

Mom

Did you ever have any unusual hobbies?

What movies or cartoons did you watch when you were young?

Daughter

What are your hobbies?

____

____

____

____

Is there something that worries you that you'd like to talk about?

____

____

____

____

Mom

Did you ever have to make a tough decision as a kid?

____

____

____

____

What do you love doing now when you have free time?

____

____

____

____

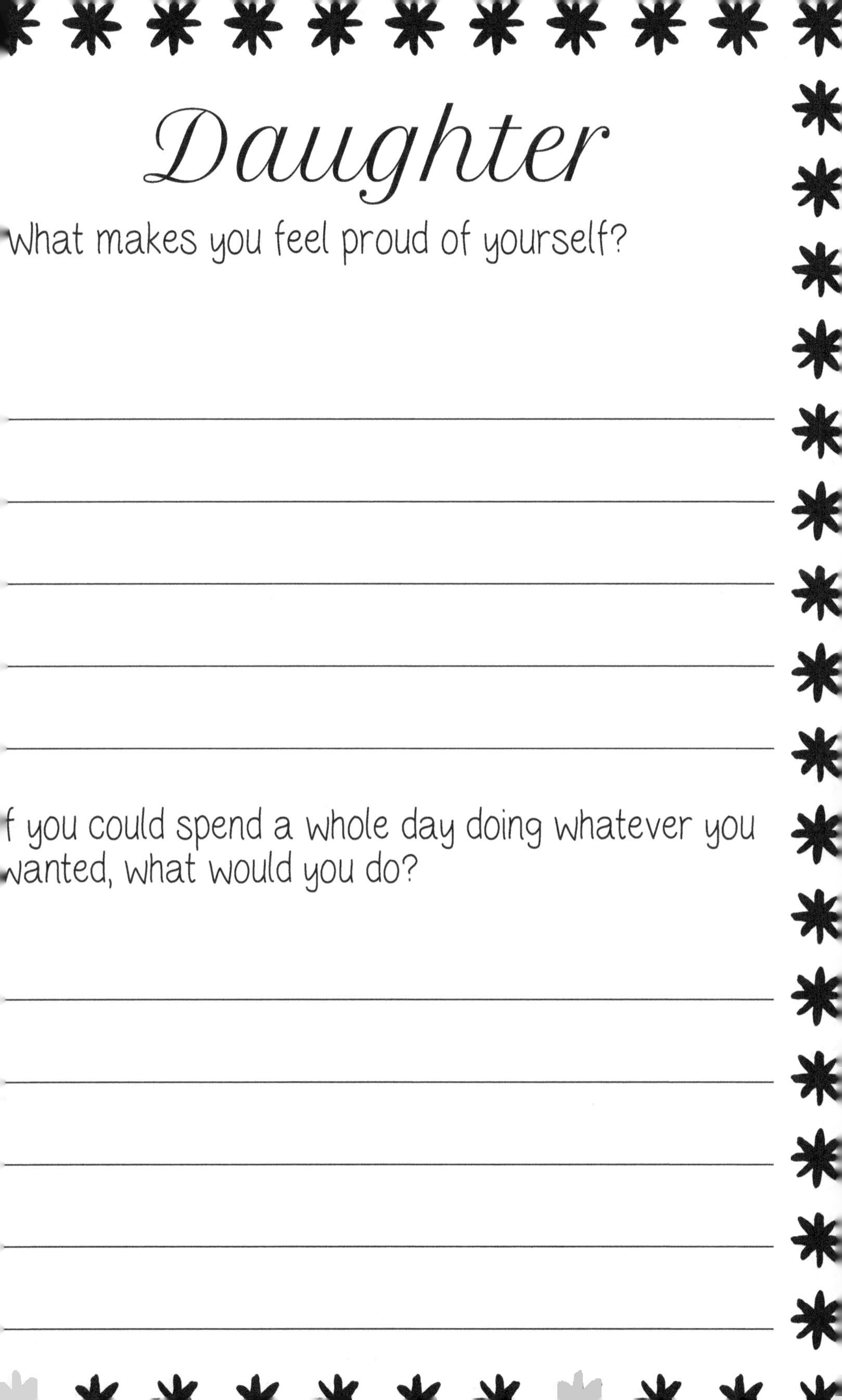

Daughter

What makes you feel proud of yourself?

____

____

____

____

f you could spend a whole day doing whatever you
wanted, what would you do?

____

____

____

____

What has been the biggest challenge you've ha
to face?
ME
MOM

What do you wish others knew about you but rarely talk about?
MOM
ME

Mom

The person I went to with my worries when I was young was...

____

____

____

____

If I ever want to talk about my feelings, I solemnly swear to talk to you or...

____

____

____

____

Signature: _______________________________________

Daughter

The person I will go to with my worries will be...

____

____

____

____

If I ever want to talk about my feelings,
I solemnly swear that I will talk to you or...

____

____

____

____

Signature: _______________________________

Mom

What do you think makes you such a warm and wise person?

1

2

3

Daughter

What do you think makes you unique and strong?

1

2

3

Mom

The time and place I was born is...

____

____

My most memorable birthday is...

____

____

My favorite ever present was...

____

____

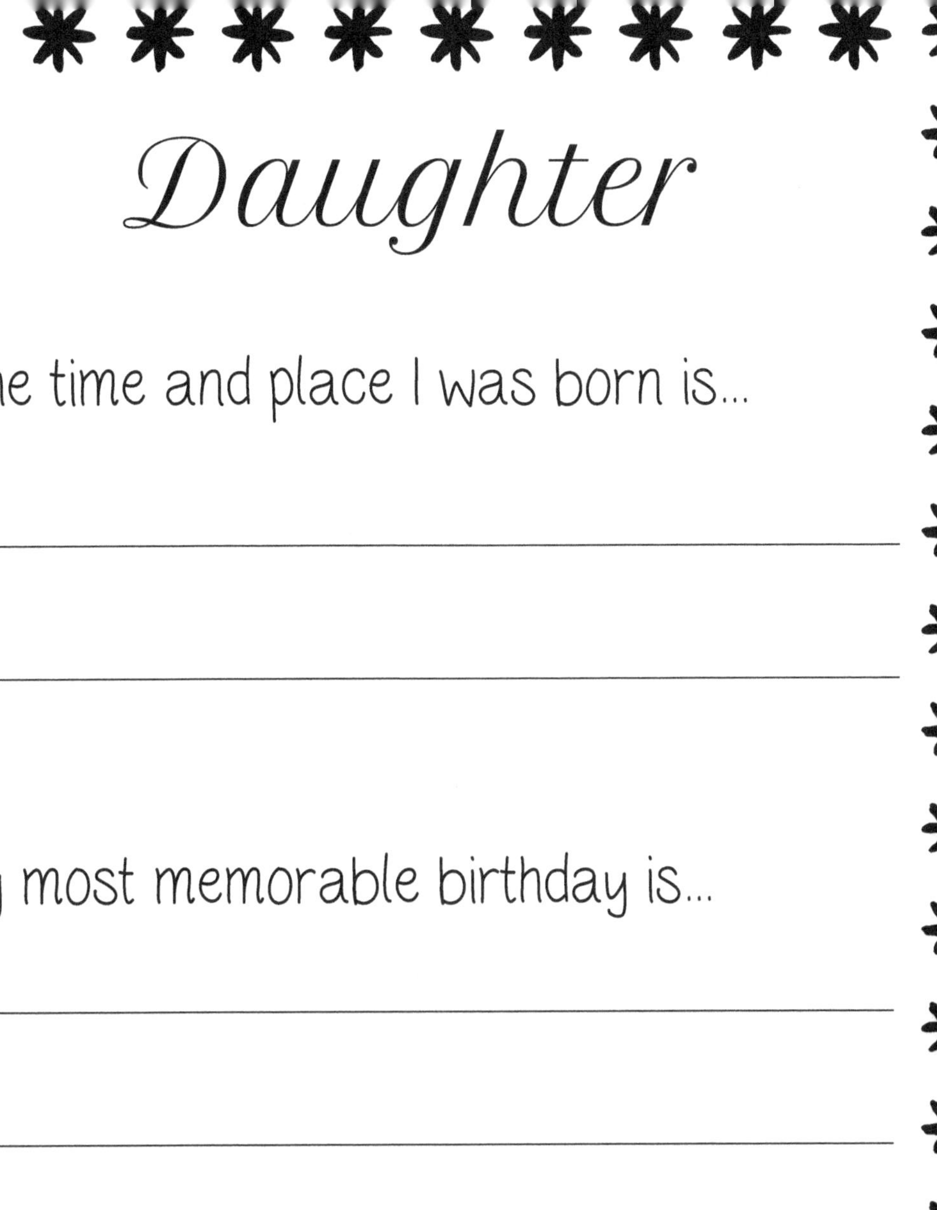

Daughter

The time and place I was born is...

____

____

My most memorable birthday is...

____

____

My favorite ever present was...

____

____

Family Photos

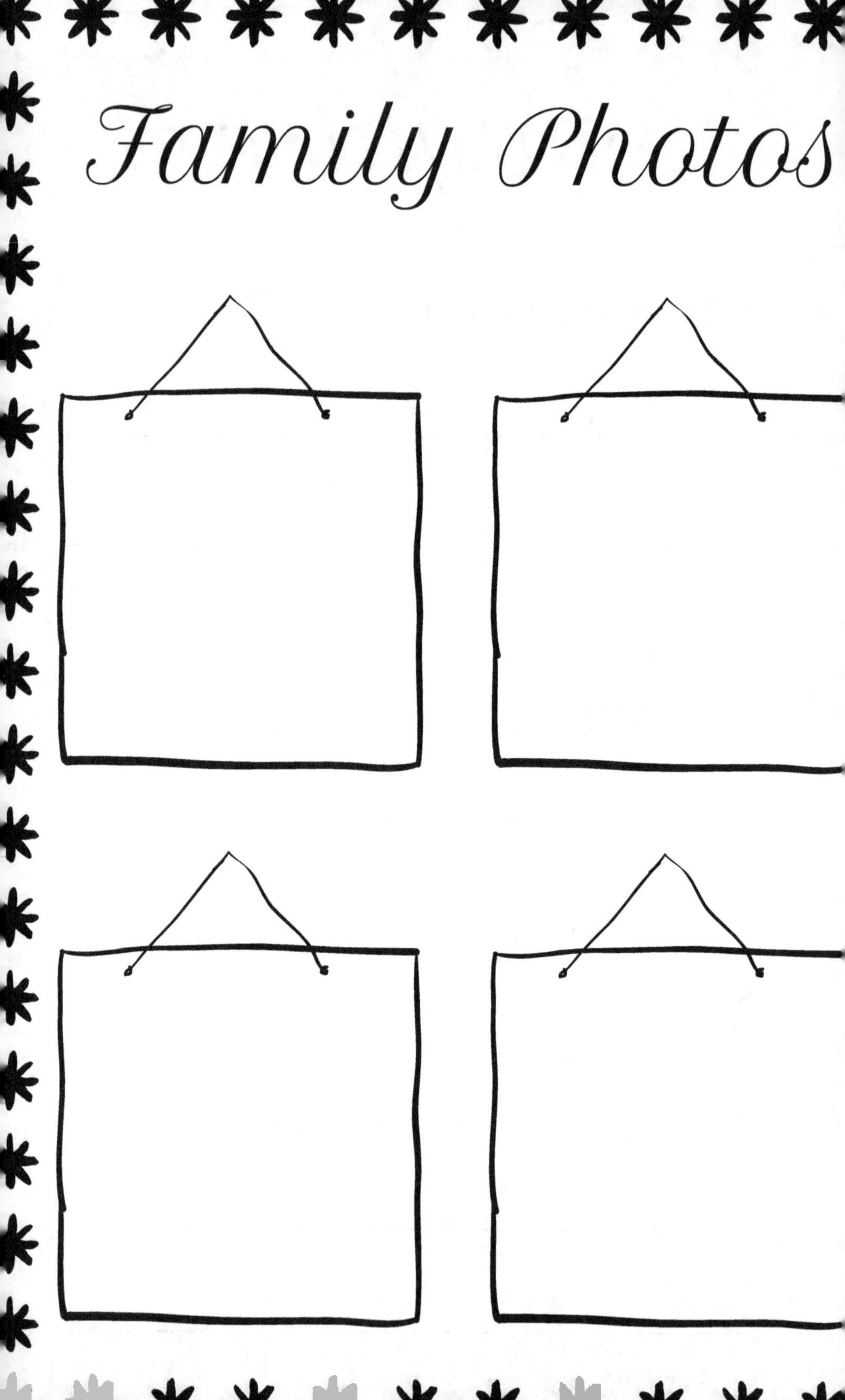

Family Photos

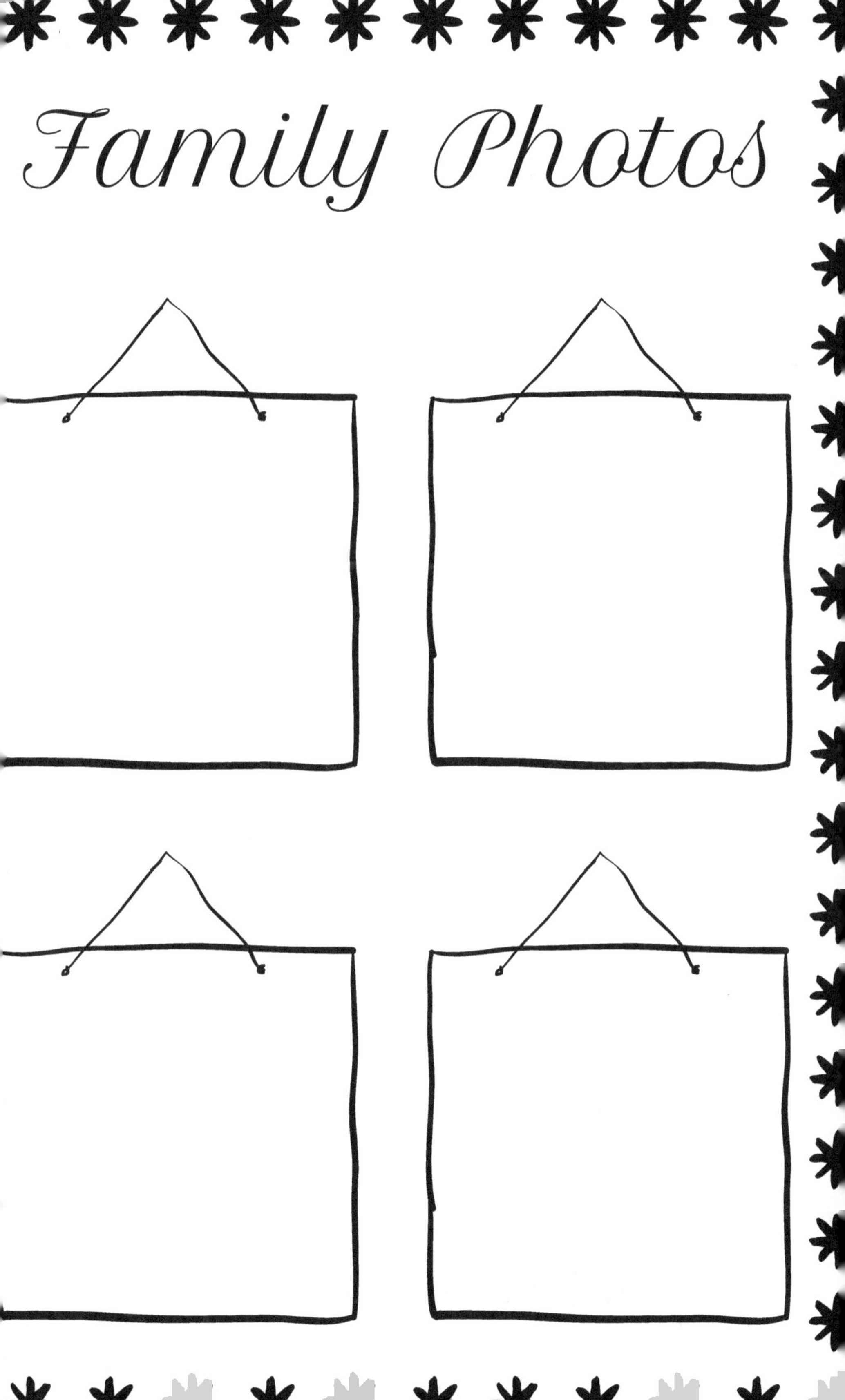

Mom

What is it about you that always makes me feel loved and safe?

Daughter

What is it that you do that always makes me proud of you?

____

____

____

____

____

____

____

____

____

Mom

If I could have three wishes, they would be...

1

2

3

Daughter

If I could have three wishes, they would be...

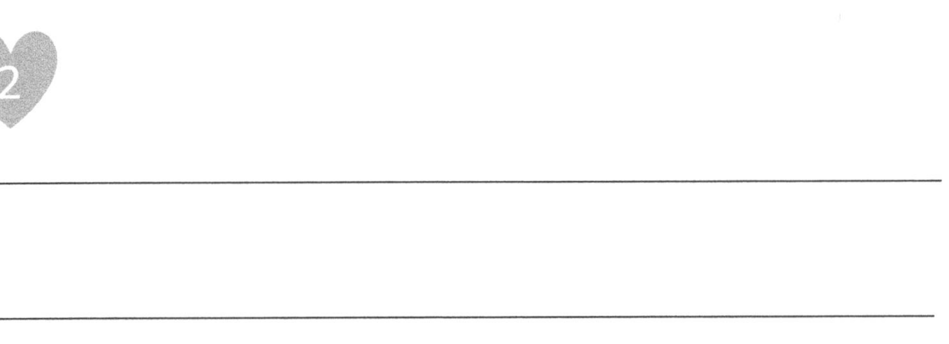

Mom

What do you think makes our relationship so strong?

1

2

3

Daughter

What is something about you that makes our bond so special?

1

2

3

Mom

If I could imagine myself in an amazing outfit that would make me feel more confident when I'm feeling anxious, it would look like...

Daughter

Daughter... When you feel anxious or lack confidence, imagine yourself in an amazing outfit. Everyone thinks you look wonderful. Draw a picture and describe what it looks like...

Mom

Mom, tell me about the strangest dream you've ever had

Daughter

Daughter, tell me about the strangest dream you've ever had...

Mom

This is Mom,
he looks happy...

This is Mom
being silly

Daughter

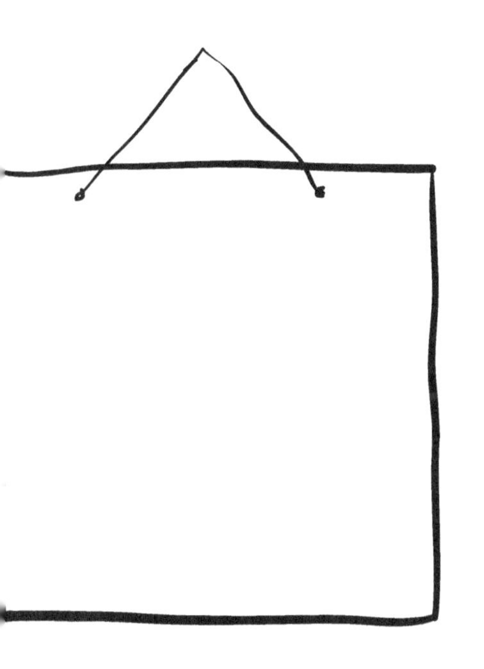

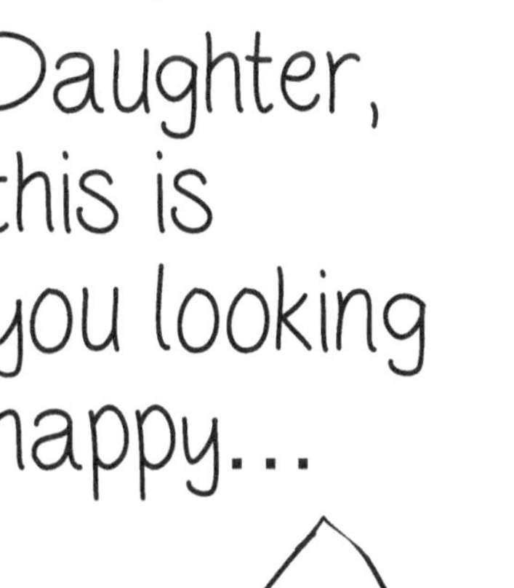

Daughter,
this is
you looking
happy...

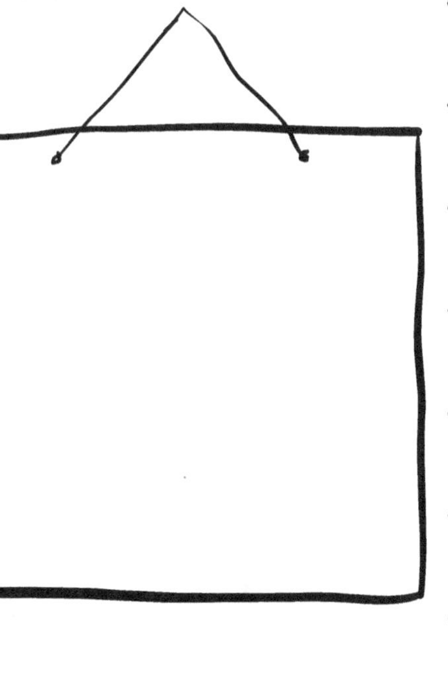

Daughter,
this is
you being silly...

Mom

If I could have three superpowers, they would be...

1

____

____

2

____

____

3

____

____

Daughter

If I could have three superpowers, they would be...

1

2

3

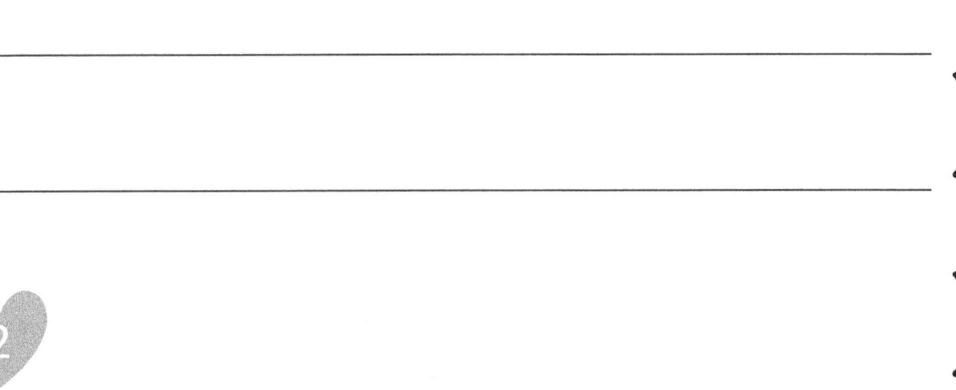

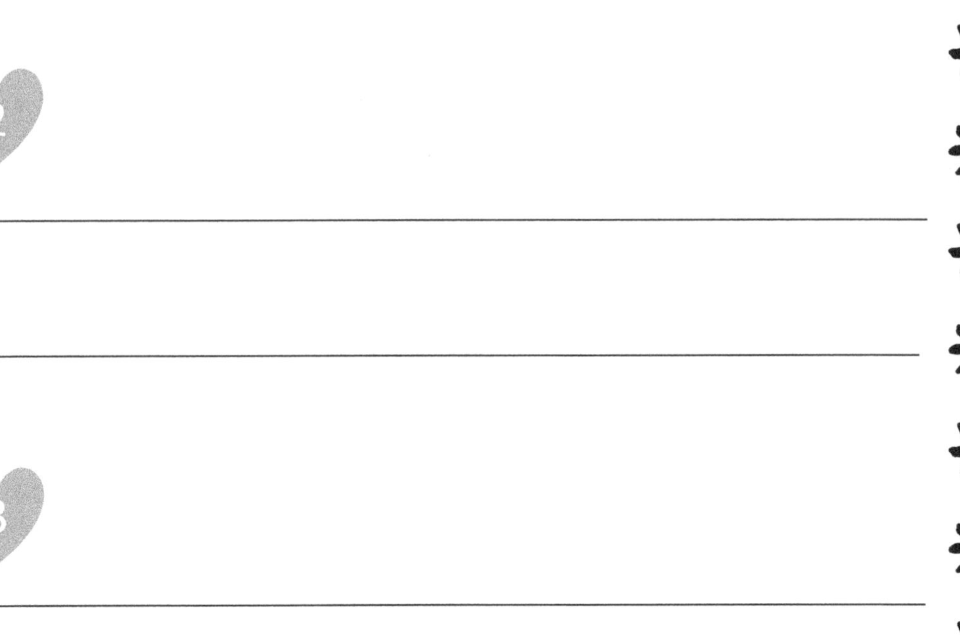

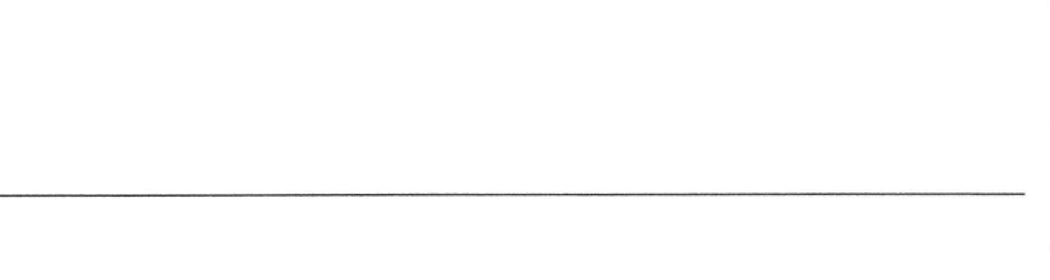

Mom

My best friends as a child were...

____

____

____

My best friends now are...

____

____

____

What I've learned about friendships are...

____

____

____

Daughter

My best friends are...

____

____

____

The things I like best about my friends are...

____

____

____

The things I don't like about my friends are...

____

____

____

Mom

Mom, did you sleep with a stuffed animal when you were little? Can you tell me about it?

Daughter

My favorite cuddly toy is a __________ called __________.
I will never throw it away because...

Mom
My top 10 songs of all time are...
Tunes
1.
2.
3.
4.
5.
6.
7.
8.
9.
10.

Daughter

My favourite top 10 songs are...

1. _______________________________________

2. _______________________________________

3. _______________________________________

4. _______________________________________

5. _______________________________________

6. _______________________________________

7. _______________________________________

8. _______________________________________

9. _______________________________________

10. _______________________________________

Mom

Mom, tell me about something kind you did for someone...

Daughter

Daughter, tell me about something kind you did for someone...

Mom

If you could have dinner with anyone in the world-past or present-who would it be and why?

Daughter

If you could spend an entire day doing anything, what would your perfect day look like?

Mom

Other Things I Want To Say To You,

Daughter

Other Things I Want To Say To You,

Mom

Other Things I Want To Say To You,

Daughter

Other Things I Want To Say To You,

Dear Mom and Beloved Daughter,

As you reach the end of this shared journey through the pages of this journal, I want you both to remember the special time you spent together. Every conversation, question, and answer has built a foundation of love, mutual respect, and understanding between you. The memories you've shared here are not only a record of your history but also a testament to the incredible bond you have, growing stronger with each passing day.

Mom, your wisdom and life experiences are invaluable. By sharing them, you have given your daughter a treasure that will stay with her forever. Your stories, advice, and love will accompany her through every stage of life. Your words are not just memories from the past but also guiding lights for the future.

Daughter, your questions and curiosity show how much you want to know and understand your mother, and how deeply you value her presence in your life. Every conversation has been an opportunity to grow closer, to build memories together that will become a precious legacy for years to come.

Let this journal be a reminder of the importance of family bonds, of nurturing closeness, and of continually discovering new sides of each other. May your conversations never end, and may the love you've written down here be seen every day in your gestures, words, and shared moments. What you have created will endure for generations and become a cherished keepsake for you and your family.

We hope this journal marks the beginning of even more shared moments and conversations that will last a lifetime. The memories you have captured here will always be with you, and each new conversation will fill your hearts with joy and love.